WORLD OF READING

WORKBOOK

OUT CAME THE ·SUN·

P. DAVID PEARSON   DALE D. JOHNSON

THEODORE CLYMER   ROSELMINA INDRISANO   RICHARD L. VENEZKY

JAMES F. BAUMANN   ELFRIEDA HIEBERT   MARIAN TOTH

Consulting Authors

CARL GRANT   JEANNE PARATORE

SILVER BURDETT & GINN

NEEDHAM, MA • MORRISTOWN, NJ
ATLANTA, GA • CINCINNATI, OH • DALLAS, TX
MENLO PARK, CA • NORTHFIELD, IL

TABLE OF CONTENTS

ISBN 0-663-46165-0

NAME _____

Down   Out   up   up

The itsy bitsy spider

_____

went _____ up _____ the waterspout.

_____

_ _ _ _ _ _ _ _ _ _ _ _ _

_____ came the rain
and washed the spider out.

_____

_ _ _ _ _ _ _ _ _ _ _ _ _

_____ came the sun
and dried up all the rain.

And the itsy bitsy spider

_____

_ _ _ _ _ _ _ _ _ _ _ _

went _____ the spout again.

Take-Home Book   ''The Itsy Bitsy Spider''
Have children write a word from the box to finish each sentence. Then have them color in the picture.

3

"The Itsy Bitsy Spider"
Have children number the pictures from 1 to 4 to retell the story of the itsy bitsy spider.

Take-Home Book

4

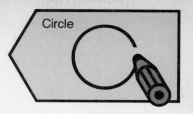
NAME _____

1.

2.

3.

4.

COMPREHENSION: Cause/Effect
Have children look at each box on the left. This box is the cause. Then have children circle the picture on the right that answers the question "What happened?"

"Rain"

5

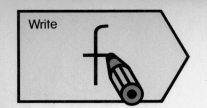

Write

down　out　rain　up

Will it __rain__ ?

You can put _____ your .

The sun has come _____ .

Ed, put your _____ .

"Rain"
Have children look at each picture and write a word from the box to finish the sentence.

Selection Vocabulary

6

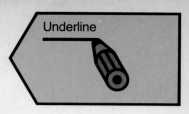
NAME _____

It looks like rain.

The sun is out.

The sun is up in the sky.

2.

The rain will not fall down.

Put up your umbrella.

Put down your umbrella.

3.

It looks like rain.

Put down your umbrella.

The sun is not out.

4.

Put up your umbrella.

What do you see in the sky?

I can see the rain.

Selection Comprehension   "Rain"
Have children retell the story by drawing a line under the sentence that goes with each picture.

7

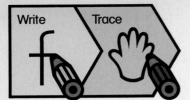

Write Trace

ca**p**   bo**x**

p

6

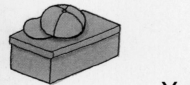

Your ca____ is on the bo____ .

"Rain"
Have children name each picture and write *p* or *x* for the final sound. Then have them trace and complete the sentence at the bottom.

DECODING AND WORD STUDY: Final Consonants   p, x

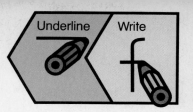

Meg and Max **look** up at the sky.

The cat **looks** up at the sky.

see
<u>sees</u>

1. Max ___**sees**___ a .

see
sees

2. Meg and the cat _____ a .

like
likes

3. The cat _____ the  .

find
finds

4. The dog _____ the cat.

DECODING AND WORD STUDY: *Inflection -s* with Verbs

"Rain"

Have children draw a line under the word from the box that goes in each sentence and then write the word in the blank.

1. The rain came down.

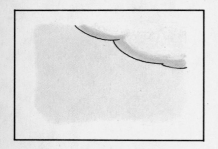  

2. The truck went through the rain.

3. The dog did not look out for the truck.

4. The sun came out.

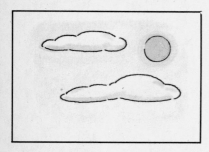  

"Rain"
Have children read the matching sentence above the first picture and circle the picture that answers the question "What happened?".

COMPREHENSION: Cause/Effect

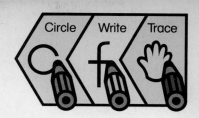

Circle Write Trace

pin

pin

f__n

p__g

p__t

The ___ p__g ___ has a ___ w__g ___.

DECODING AND WORD STUDY: Short *i* /i/   **"Out in the Rain"**
Have children circle pictures of words with short *i*, fill in the letter, and trace the word. Have them complete the
sentence at the bottom.

11

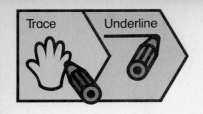

Trace   Underline

in my said with

1.

Ted said, "I can't fix my cap."

Ted is with his mom, too.

2.

Dad said, "Is it my cap?"

Dad said, "Put it in here."

3.

I will get my umbrella.

The cap is with the umbrella.

4.

Ted said, "Dad did fix my cap, too."

Dad said, "I can't fix it."

"Out in the Rain"
Have children trace the story words at the top and underline the sentence that goes with each picture.

Circle

1. Look at the sky. It looks like _____ .

2. _____ said, "Will you go out in the rain with me?"

3. Gram said, "Hold on to your _____ !"

4. Tim said, "Can you fix my _____ ?"

5. Tim said, "I like what you did to my _____ ."

Selection Comprehension
Have children retell the story by circling a picture to complete each sentence.

"Out in the Rain"

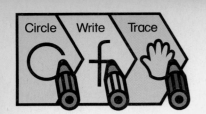

Circle Write Trace

ca**b**

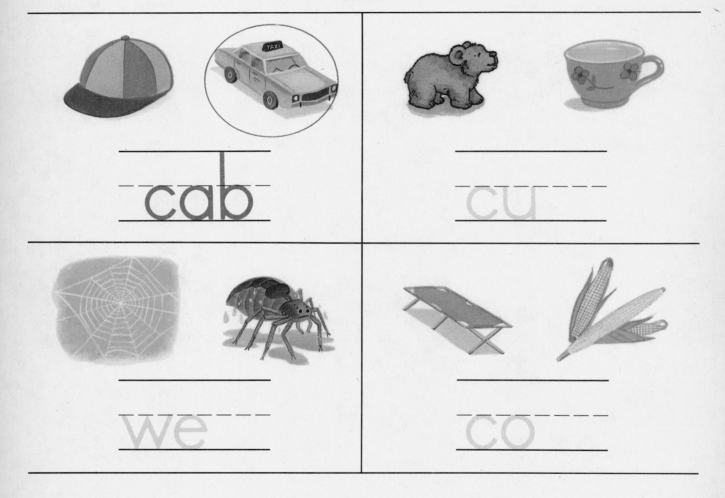

cab

cu

we

co

The _____ cu is in a _____ ca .

"Out in the Rain"   **DECODING AND WORD STUDY: Final Consonant b /b/**
Have children circle pictures of words that end with b, fill in the letter, and trace the word. Have them complete the sentence at the bottom.

NAME _____

pin

| fix | in | wind | with |

1.

Can you __fix__ this for me?

2.

I put _____ a pin.

3.

Hold on and run _____ it.

4.

Run like the _____ !

DECODING AND WORD STUDY: Short *i* /i/
Have children look at each picture and write a word from the box to finish the sentence.

"Out in the Rain"

15

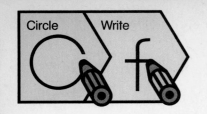

Circle | Write

ca**p**

bo**x**

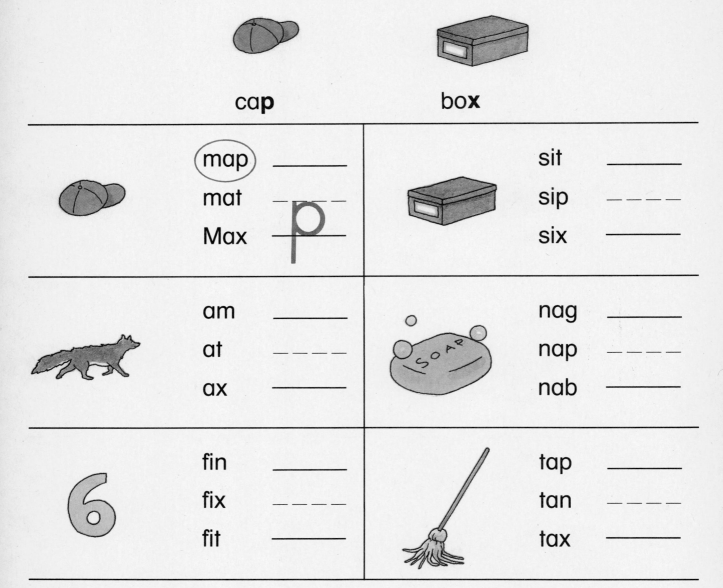

(map) _____
mat _____
Max **p**

sit _____
sip _ _ _ _ _
six _____

am _____
at _ _ _ _ _
ax _____

nag _____
nap _ _ _ _ _
nab _____

fin _____
fix _ _ _ _ _
fit _____

tap _____
tan _ _ _ _ _
tax _____

Can you __fi_____ my __ca_____ ?

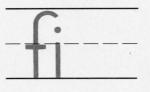

"Out in the Rain"
Have children circle the word that ends with the same sound as the name of the picture and write *p* or *x*. Then have them complete the sentence at the bottom.

DECODING AND WORD STUDY: Final Consonants *p, x*

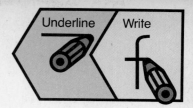

Underline / Write

NAME _____

| get |
| gets |

| hold |
| holds |

| ride |
| rides |

| like |
| likes |

| look |
| looks |

1. Gram **gets** an umbrella.

2. Tim _____ on to Gram.

3. Gram and Tim _____ in the sky.

4. Tim _____ to ride with Gram.

5. Tim and Gram _____ happy.

DECODING AND WORD STUDY: Inflection -s with Verbs   **"Out in the Rain"**
Have children draw a line under the word from the box that goes in each sentence and then write the word in the blank.

17

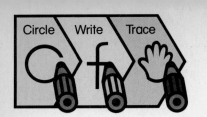

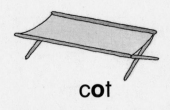

cot

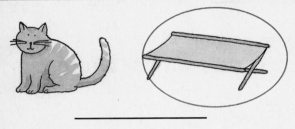

cot

c _ b

 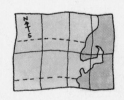

m _ p

p _ t

Is the p _ t on the c _ t ?

"What a Surprise!"
Have children circle pictures of words with short o, fill in the letter, and trace the word. Have them complete the sentence at the bottom.

DECODING AND WORD STUDY: Short *o* /o/

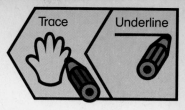

NAME _____

have jump make went

1.

Tim and Gram went to the  .

Tim and Gram have a surprise.

2.

Gram will make a cap.

Gram said, "I have a lot of  .

3.

Tim said, "I can not jump."

Tim said, "I like to jump."

4.

Gram said, "You and I can make a web."

Gram and Tim like to jump a lot.

Selection Vocabulary
Have children trace the story words at the top and underline the sentence that goes with each picture.

"What a Surprise!"

19

1. The _____ was blowing.

    rain   sun   (wind)

2. _____ went up in the sky.

    Nat   Bitsy   Tim

3. Nat did not like it _____ there.

    out   down   up

4. Bitsy said, "I will make a _____ for you."

    cap   web   ride

5. Nat had to _____ down.

    ride   jump   hop

6. Nat was _____ to have a web to jump on.

    sad   mad   happy

"What a Surprise!"
Have children retell the story by circling a word to finish each sentence.

20

Selection Comprehension

Write

cot

| box | lot | not | top |

1.

Nat said, "Look at this __box__ .

2.

Bitsy said, "What is at the _____ ?"

3.

Nat said, "I like the surprise a _____ !"

4.

Bitsy said, "I do _____ like it at all!"

DECODING AND WORD STUDY: Short *o* /o/   "What a Surprise!"
Have children look at each picture and write a word from the box to finish the sentence.

21

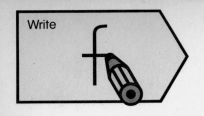

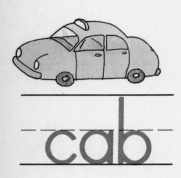

cab

we

De

cu

1. I like the tan ___cub___ .

2. Get in the big _____ .

3. Bitsy has a big _____ .

4. Bob and _____ can jump.

"What a Surprise!"   **DECODING AND WORD STUDY: Final Consonant** *b* **/b/**
Have children identify each picture and write the name below it. Then have them write the missing word to complete each sentence.

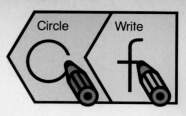

NAME _____

pin

with

1. What can I do (with) the pan?

2. I have it!

3. I can jump around the rim.

4. I can make a big surprise for Nat.

5. What is the surprise?

DECODING AND WORD STUDY: Short *i* /i/
Have children find, circle, and write each word that has the short *i* sound.

"What a Surprise!"

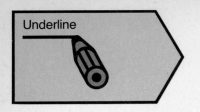

1. The wind was blowing.

The sun was out.

There was no rain.

Nat went up and up.

2. Bitsy will help Nat.

Bitsy will jump up.

Bitsy will make a web.

Bitsy did get to Nat.

3. Nat did jump.

Nat went down.

Nat went up.

Nat went out.

4. Nat did jump on the web.

Nat went down again.

Nat went up again.

Nat went out again.

"What a Surprise!"
Have children read the sentence above the picture and underline the sentence that answers the question "What happened?".

COMPREHENSION: Cause/Effect

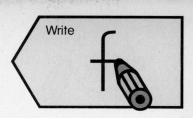

! . ? " "

1. Look up in the sky [.]

2. What do you see [ ]

3. Bitsy said, "Do you like it [ ] "

4. Nat said, [ ] I do. [ ]

5. What a surprise [ ]

WORD STUDY: Punctuation
Have children fill in the correct punctuation mark.

"Marks"

25

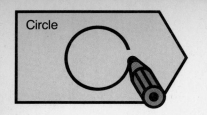
1. s<u>i</u>t     **10**

2. h<u>o</u>p

3. bo<u>x</u>

4. ta<u>p</u>    **6**

5. _____ jump up and down.

   Gram   Nat   Nat and Bitsy

6. _____ jumps up and down.

   Gram and Tim   Nat   Nat and Bitsy

At the top, have children read each word and circle the picture or pictures whose names have the same sound as the underlined letter. At the bottom, have children circle the word or words that can go in the sentence. Point out that there may be more than one answer.

Draw

NAME _____

The bear went over the mountain.
The bear went over the mountain.
The bear went over the mountain,
to see what he could see.

The other side of the mountain,
the other side of the mountain,
the other side of the mountain,
was all that he could see.

Take-Home Book
Have children read the song and finish the picture by drawing what the bear could see.

"The Bear Went Over the Mountain"

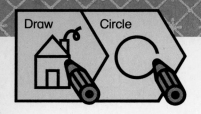

I went over the mountain
to see what I could see.

Put what you can see on the mountain.

"The Bear Went Over the Mountain"   **Take-Home Book**
Have children draw pictures of things they could see on a mountain. Have them circle each picture after drawing it.

NAME _____

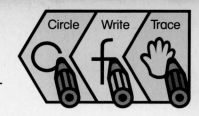

cub

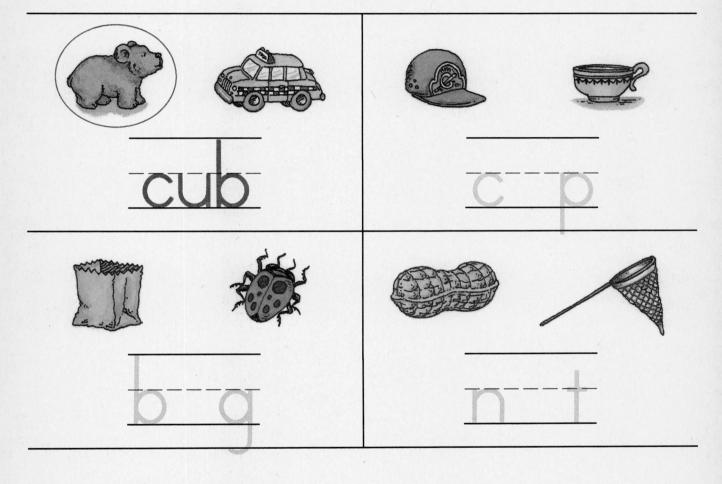

cub

c __ p

b __ g

n __ t

The c __ b went __ __ p .

DECODING AND WORD STUDY: Short _u_ /u/
Have children circle pictures whose names have the short _u_ sound, fill in the letter, and trace the word. Have them complete the sentence at the bottom.

"Up and Down the Mountain"

Write

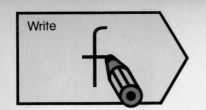

fun of side mountain

1.

Go up the _mountain_ .

2.

Go to the top _____ the mountain.

3.

Go down the other _____ .

This is _____ !

"Up and Down the Mountain"
Have children look at each picture and write a word from the box to finish the sentence.

Selection Vocabulary

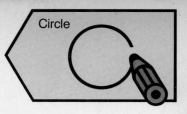

NAME _____

1. Go up the side of the mountain and see _____ .

---

2. See _____ at the top of the mountain.

---

3. Go down the other side and see _____ .

---

4. What can you see on the mountain?

Selection Comprehension
Have children retell the story by circling a picture to answer each question.

"Up and Down the Mountain"

31

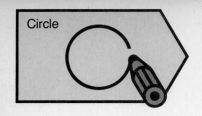

1. You can find me in my den with my cub.
What am I?

2. You can go up and down the mountain with me.
What am I?

3. I went up the mountain.
What did I see?

4. You can see that I got to the top of the mountain.
What did I do?

"Up and Down the Mountain"
COMPREHENSION: Inference
Have children read the sentence and use what they know to circle the picture that answers each question.

32

Write

 c**u**b

fun   run   sun   up

1.

It is hot in the ___sun___ .

2.

This is not _____ .

3.

I can not _____ .

4.

See you _____ at the top!

DECODING AND WORD STUDY: Short *u* /u/   **"Up and Down the Mountain"**
Have children look at each picture and write a word from the box to finish the sentence.

33

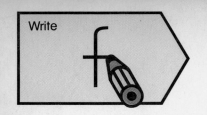
Write

ca**p**

| Max   up   box |
| Max   map |

bo**x**

1. Max got out his _____ .

2. He went _____ the mountain.

3. He sat on a _____ .

4. _____ had fun on the mountain.

"Up and Down the Mountain"   DECODING AND WORD STUDY: Final Consonants *p, x*
Have children write a word from the box to finish each sentence.

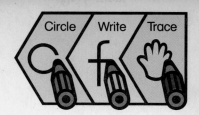
NAME _____

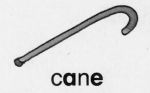

cane

cane

m__ne

v__ne

c__pe

Have a ___ c__pe ___ and a ___ c__ne ___ .

DECODING AND WORD STUDY: Long *a* /ā/
Have children circle pictures whose names have the long *a* sound, fill in the letter, and trace the word. Have them complete the sentence at the bottom.

"The Sand Mountain"

35

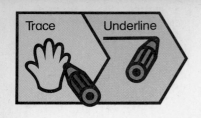
all came over play

1.

The sun came out.

The sun went down.

2.

The bear went over the mountain.

The bear got off the mountain.

3.

Will the bear nap?

Who will play with him?

4.

The cat will play.

All of us will play.

"The Sand Mountain"   **Selection Vocabulary**
Have children trace the story words at the top and underline the sentence that goes with each picture.

NAME _____

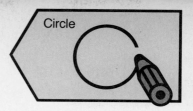
1. Mom said to make a _____ .

  (mountain of sand)   mud cake   surprise

2. Jane came to _____ .

  play with Mom   get Fran   help Bob

3. Fran came to _____ with Bob and Jane.

  ride   run   play

4. Fran put _____ on the sand.

  wind   water   an umbrella

5. Bob, Jane, and Fran made the mountain _____ .

  hot   big   fall

6. Bob _____ Jane and Fran.

  had fun with   made a cake for   did not help

Selection Comprehension
Have children retell the story by circling a word or phrase to finish each sentence.

"The Sand Mountain"

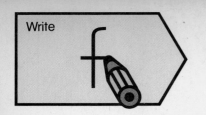
| came | Jane | made | wave |

cane

1.

Jane **came** to play with Bob.

2.

Jane and Bob _____ a mountain.

3.

A _____ washed it out.

4.

_____ and Bob put it up again.

"The Sand Mountain"
Have children look at each picture and write a word from the box to finish the sentence.

DECODING AND WORD STUDY: Long *a* /ā/

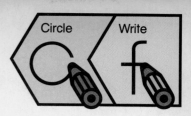

NAME _____

cub

1. Come with (us.)

2. Come out in the sun.

3. Take a cup of water.

4. Make a mud cake.

5. This is fun!

us

DECODING AND WORD STUDY: Short *u* /u/
Have children find, circle, and write each word that has the short *u* sound as in *cub*.

"The Sand Mountain"

39

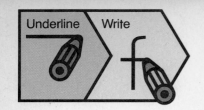

Underline | Write

| make |
| makes |

| jump |
| jumps |

| jump |
| jumps |

| play |
| plays |

| run |
| runs |

1. The sun **makes** the sand hot.

_____

2. Bob _____ in the water.

_____

3. Jane and Fran _____ in, too.

_____

4. Bob, Jane, and Fran _____ .

_____

5. A dog _____ in and plays, too.

"The Sand Mountain" **DECODING AND WORD STUDY: Inflection -s with Verbs**
Have children draw a line under the word from the box that goes in each sentence and then write the word in the blank.

Write

| Bud | Bob | wheel | Fran | Bob |

1. Fran said to Bob, "Ride to Bear Mountain with **me**."

Fran

2. Bob said, "**I** can not go. Look at my wheel."

3. Fran said, "Bud can fix **it**."

4. Bob said, "Who is **he**?"

5. Fran said, "**You** will see."

Selection Comprehension
Have children read the words in the box. Then have them read each sentence and write the word from the box that tells who or what the word in dark type stands for.

"Bear Mountain"

41

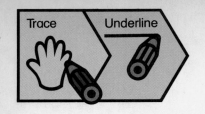

Trace → Underline

bears could he
live they

1.

Who could live there?

There is a bear.

2.

I do!

Look, they do!

3.

The bear is big.

That is a den of bears.

4.

Is he the bear cub?

They could not see a cub.

"Bear Mountain"

Selection Vocabulary

Have children trace the story words at the top and underline the sentence that goes with each picture.

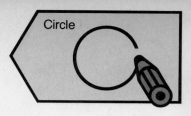

Circle

1. The 3 bears, the cat, and the dog did not
_____ in the cave.
live   (fit)   plan

2. K.C. went over _____ .
Sand Mountain   Dog Lake   Bear Mountain

3. He came to D.D. with a _____ .
plan   box   cave

4. K.C. and D.D. fix up the _____ .
plan   box   cave

5. They all _____ the cave they live in.
get out of   like   do not fit in

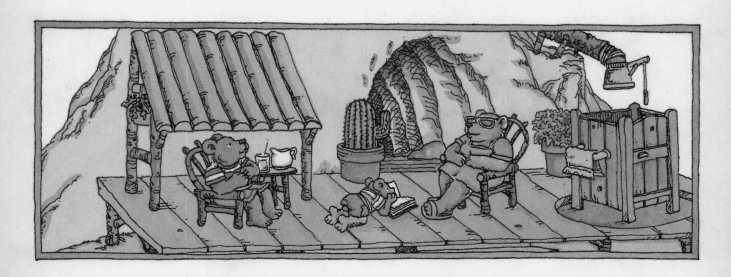

Selection Comprehension
Have children retell the story by circling a word or phrase to finish each sentence.

"Bear Mountain"

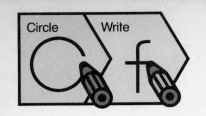

cot

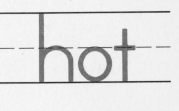

1. The cave was too (hot.)

2. The bear cub could not take a nap.

3. K.C., D.D., and the cub went to
the mountain top.

4. K.C. put up a cot for his cub.

5. D.D. said, "I like this a lot."

"Bear Mountain"

Have children find, circle, and write each word that has the short o sound as in cot.

DECODING AND WORD STUDY: Short o/o/

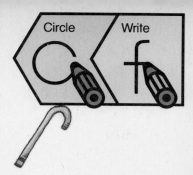
NAME _____

cane

Do this

 1. Mop the (cave.)

 cave

 2. Mix a cake.

 3. Put up a gate.

 4. Wake K.C. at 3:00.

5. Take a nap.

DECODING AND WORD STUDY: Long _a_ /ā/
Have children find, circle, and write each word that has the long _a_ sound as in _cane_..

"Bear Mountain"

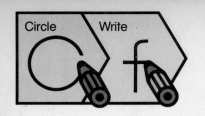
Circle   Write

ca**b**

1. K.C. could not find the (bib.)

2. The cub ate without it.

3. K.C. had to put him in the tub.

4. K.C. had to rub.

5. What a job K.C. had!

bib

"Bear Mountain"   **DECODING AND WORD STUDY: Final Consonant** *b* /b/
Have children find, circle, and write each word that ends with the same sound as *cab*.

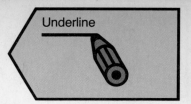

NAME _____

1.

K.C. has a plan.

D.D. can help.

K.C. and D.D. fix up the cave.

2.

K.C. is at bat.

K.C. and D.D. play a game with B.J.

D.D. will run.

3.

The Bears have fun in the sun.

The umbrella is up.

K.C. plays with the dog.

4.

D.D. is hot.

The cat looks around.

The Bears go for a ride.

COMPREHENSION: Main Idea/Picture Details   **"What Is It About?"**
Have children look at each picture and underline the sentence that tells what the whole picture is about.

Circle

1. c<u>u</u>p

2. m<u>a</u>k<u>e</u>

3. we<u>b</u>

4.

5.

Checkpoint

At the top, have children read each word and circle the pictures whose names have the same sound as the underlined letters. At the bottom, have children circle the picture that answers the question "What happened?".

MNOPQR - W - 98 97 96 95 94 93